Change the world. Start with the children.

Words from Father William Wasson, whose legacy—raising over 20,000 orphaned and vulnerable children—lives on at Nuestros Pequeños Hermanos.

Father William Wasson
with Bishop Ronald Hicks & Marlene Farrell Byrne

Library of Congress Catalog Number: 2020902554
Library of Congress Cataloging-in-Publication Data

Change the World. Start with the Children.
By: Father William Wasson, Bishop Ronald Hicks &
Marlene Farrell Byrne
ISBN: 978-0-9777135-6-1

Printed in the United State of America.

Original manuscript by Father William Wasson
translated by Janet Chavez.
Minor children's names have been altered.
Many contributors have helped create this book—
please forgive any inconsistencies.

Big things sometimes have small beginnings.

A question. A meeting. A chance.
In that single moment,
one has the opportunity to say
"YES."

We hope this book inspires you
to say yes and change the world.

This book is dedicated to the entire
Nuestros Pequeños Hermanos family.

The children, the staff and the donors—
because this family
is changing the world.

ALL the proceeds from this book go to
NPH USA for the children.

Table of Contents

FOREWORD

By: Bishop Ronald Hicks
NPH Volunteer, Regional Director and
Auxiliary Bishop of Chicago

*"The love you have shared with countless
numbers of children has most certainly
enriched the world. You have blessed
their lives far beyond what any material
wealth could do for them; for you
have given them love, hope, faith...and care."*

—Pope John Paul II on Father Wasson

Father Wasson & Ron in 1989

No Poor, Little Me

UPON GRADUATING from college in 1989, I was without plans for the future. A priest recommended that I volunteer at a place called Nuestros Pequeños Hermanos (NPH) in Mexico. I knew nothing about Father Wasson or his work. I really just wanted to learn Spanish and thought the volunteer experience would help me decide my next move.

I was quickly indoctrinated in the extraordinary place called NPH. It was nothing like I had imagined. As opposed to the orphanage or institution environment I was expecting, this was a place structured as a family. Yes, there were problems but I was overwhelmed with how unique and effective the home was. The children were so happy it jolted me.

When I learned I would meet Father Wasson, who was returning from his travels, I could not wait. In my short time, I had listened to countless stories of his relationship with the children and his work running NPH. He had been fundraising outside of Mexico and I was anxious to see just what this bigger-than-life founder of the home was really like. What was it that made him so special?

On the day of our first meeting, I was 22 years old, not yet a priest and in my third month of volunteering at NPH. I remember sitting in the meeting room in Casa Nolan, the house Father Wasson lived in when he was in Mexico. He had requested the staff and volunteers come to update him on activities in the home. When the doors opened, there was silence and everyone stood. You could feel the excitement and adoration in the room.

My Spanish was still limited, so I missed much of the content of the conversation between Father Wasson and the staff. I spent my time watching his body language and interactions. What greatly impacted me was the way Father Wasson listened intently to every question, comment and criticism. It was evident he was deeply concerned about what was being discussed and consistently responded in a soft, humble manner which exuded intelligence and wisdom.

From the beginning, it was clear Father Wasson was a force. I remember thinking to myself at the time, "This man is going to be a Saint one day." At the end of the meeting, I asked if he would let me take a picture with him. He graciously accepted. That photo was taken in Cuernavaca, Mexico in September, 1989 and I still treasure it today.

After this meeting, Father Wasson served us lunch and I noticed he ate last. This was one of his trademarks; always looking for ways to demonstrate the importance of serving others instead of being served.

Father Wasson began NPH without all the resources of psychologists or other professionals. He often talked about how he developed his ideas for raising children. He let his children experience their mistakes. I remember a story about a child who stole a peanut butter and jelly sandwich. He walked by Father Wasson, who knew what was hidden under his shirt. Instead of calling out his crime, Father Wasson grabbed the boy, told him he was loved and hugged him so tight the jelly squished on his skin. After a few giggles, the boy confessed and Father Wasson talked to him about the consequence of stealing. He knew how to show his children the right path while never letting them doubt his unconditional love.

Father Wasson had a way of guiding children, especially those with very difficult backgrounds. One expression he often used was "No Poor Little Me." He told the children that they must own their bad experiences, it made them who they are. They could wish it never happened but they could not wallow in it. He made them understand that everyone has bad things in their lives and the only way out was forward. He would say, "Spend your time loving and serving others and you will be happy." And, the children of NPH are happy.

He never failed to remind us that NPH is not another NGO (non-government organization) or institution. Instead, it is a family that includes not only the children, but the staff, volunteers, community and donors. The NPH family continues to RAISE CHILDREN and TRANSFORM LIVES by following his simple principles of UNCONDITIONAL LOVE, SHARING, WORK, RESPONSIBILITY and EDUCATION.

In 2005, I began a five-year term as Regional Director of NPH Central America, spending a lot of time with Father Wasson. Since then, I have stayed connected to the NPH family in many ways, from frequent trips with family and friends back to the homes, to serving on various boards. My heart will always be called to the NPH family.

There is much history in how Father Wasson started NPH and his early acceptance to this incredible calling from God. He talked about meeting the first boy and then going back to the police station a week later to accept another eight boys. As he was leaving the station, a policeman said to him, "Be careful with these miserable little kids." He was giving Father a warning about the boys and their reputation. Father Wasson simply answered, "They are not miserable. These are my sons."

Will Father Wasson ever be canonized a Saint? Perhaps one day. But until then, may you be inspired by his life, his important principles, and these stories of hope and transformation that illustrate not only his values, but also a life well-lived and shared with others.

WHO WAS
WILLIAM B. WASSON?

*"If you want to change the world,
you have to start with the children."*

—Father William Wasson

AS A YOUNG MAN, William Wasson studied to become a priest. He received his M.A. in Law and Social Sciences at San Luis Rey University, Santa Barbara, California. Before he could be ordained, he learned he had an issue with his thyroid and upon discussion with the Bishop, it was determined he was not physically fit for life in the priesthood. To help with his disappointment, his father decided William needed a rest and gave him a $100 bill to go south to Mexico. William planned to stay only a week or two but changed his mind after falling in love with the community. He found a job and enrolled in a course in Mexican history.

After a year, William began teaching criminology at the University of the Americas and working as a counselor at the American School Foundation. He continued to attend Mass every day.

One of his teachers from the seminary in the United States, a Benedictine Monk, came to visit William and asked him an important question, "Do you still want to become a priest?" When William said yes, the monk took him to visit the Bishop of Cuernavaca who asked him for a letter about his condition from his doctor. The Bishop needed priests and if William could do the work, he would accept him.

William was ordained a priest in 1953 by the VII Bishop of Cuernavaca. He was assigned to a church in the Tepetates market district of Cuernavaca called "The Church of the Poor" and rented a small apartment nearby. Almost immediately, he instituted a daycare center for poor children.

One morning as he entered the church, the sacristan who lived above the church came running down the aisle to meet him. He explained that a thief had robbed the church's poor box the night before. In Mexico, nothing could be worse than being a "church thief."

That afternoon, the sacristan again came to Father Wasson with news that the thief had been apprehended and was in custody. Father Wasson was to go to the jail to fill out the paperwork.

Upon entering the police station, he asked if he could meet the thief. To his surprise, it was a 15-year-old boy with a tragic situation, who explained to Father Wasson that he had stolen the money because he was hungry.

Unwilling to press charges, Father Wasson went to the judge on the boy's behalf. He had made the boy promise to attend school if he could obtain his freedom and the judge granted custody. The boy would live with Father Wasson for the next four years, attend school and be the first pequeño of NPH.

Within a week, the judge had sent eight more orphaned boys to Father Wasson. With his growing family, he decided to rent an old, abandoned house, asking a parishioner to pay the first month's rent. He found used beds and took what he could to provide a home for the children. To eat, Father Wasson solicited local hotels to donate their leftover soup each evening.

In time, Father Wasson would open the home to more children. As his home grew, so did his needs. He began to travel and

talk with people in his home state of Arizona, telling stories of the children. He asked for donations to help him with his work. Father Wasson believed the best way to get people to help was to touch their hearts.

Father Wasson's achievements reflected a combination of life lessons and an idea put into action. He credited his core drive with a foundation developed during his own childhood.

Born on December 21, 1923 in Phoenix, Arizona, Father William Wasson grew up with parents dedicated to serving others. They assisted in helping delinquent children at the Jamison Farm in Arizona. The family often distributed food and clothes to the poor in neighborhoods outside of Phoenix. They took in children who had no place to go, offering them their home.

> From Father Wasson, in his words...
>
> *I don't remember when I began to understand the work of my parents as a religious deed, but I guess it must have been the day I found myself personally interested with a delinquent child.*
>
> *This was the first time that I really felt interested with someone to the extent of feeling like their problems were mine.*

Father Wasson recognized the gifts his parents had given him and wanted to ensure the children under his care would enter the world ready to build on the important principles taught in the NPH family.

He dedicated 50 years of his life to serving as a father figure, provider and teacher to over 20,000 orphaned, vulnerable and poor children. What started as a gesture of love grew to an organization dedicated to changing the lives of children in Latin America and the Caribbean forever.

Father Wasson created the NPH family with four foundational principles—love, sharing, work and responsibility. Through drive and determination, he expanded his homes to nine countries, leaving a lasting legacy that would change the world forever.

In his own words...

I would like to share with you the story of my family—Nuestros Pequeños Hermanos [Our Little Brothers and Sisters]—not because I believe to have found all the answers, but because I believe to have found some answers and I think what I have can be applied to all children who are with or without their natural family.

Our family (to say that it is mine wouldn't be right because many people have helped me in its formation) began in August of 1954 when a helpless, homeless child robbed the Church of Tepetates, in Cuernavaca, where I was the Chaplain. I asked the police for custody of the child and a few days later they brought me eight more street children who had been arrested, robbing to feed themselves.

At that time, I was a recently ordained Catholic priest. I didn't have a sufficient home, money or a place to put children; and I had no idea how I would feed, clothe, house or educate them. From the beginning, I played it by ear, so to speak. Despite the mistakes that I made; from the influx of children; the lack of money (we never have enough); it began to come clear, the concept that what makes children happy and feel sure of themselves is when they share work and are responsible.

All of this doesn't mean that I nor the NPH children feel fully satisfied, like we live in a small utopia. On the contrary, we are one family with a whole host of problems. Our philosophy is still in development. We still fail yet we are still striving. But I know that we have achieved something and this is what I want to share with you, as sincerely and simply as I can. What we have learned in NPH is that if we can change and improve the lives of children in any part of the world, then we have done something, no matter how small it is, to promote fraternity among men.

So, as we live this philosophy, it consists of a balance between four different concepts—love, sharing, work and responsibility—which, taken together, create a situation in which children are happy. What is happiness? I see it in our family as a deep tranquility; a satisfaction that the children feel about life and a positive attitude towards the future."

Today, the NPH homes still practice the foundational principles of Father Wasson. This book explores his important philosophy for raising children and showcases his unimaginable success at transforming the lives of children; creating leaders in their own countries.

PRINCIPLE ONE:
UNCONDITIONAL LOVE

Love bears all things, believes all things,
hopes all things, and endures all things.
—St. Paul 1 Corinthians 13

WHEN DEFINING LOVE, they say conditional love is earned while unconditional love is given freely, no matter the circumstance. This means unconditional love is not only a feeling but also an action. NPH's first action with any child is accepting them and their siblings without bias for their circumstance. It is this act of total acceptance that creates the basic foundation on which every child's story is built. Once part of the NPH family, the children feel the deep, unconditional love from leaders, staff and donors. They are also expected to share unconditional love with their NPH siblings and carry that love out into the world.

Father Wasson gave every NPH child his love and required staff members to spread profound love and caring to the children living in his homes. He believed that unconditional love was the first founding principle with which to build his unique family.

For those who knew Father Wasson, and even those who have only heard the stories of his legacy, there is a deep understanding of the importance and profound impact of unconditional love. Anyone connected to NPH can see how this love reaches far beyond the children in his homes. The philosophy empowers donors to share their love by supporting a home or sponsoring a child. It impacts families who carry the principle of unconditional love back home to their own children and strengthen the love they share. It is evident in the communities where NPH welcomes those most vulnerable with open arms. Love fills the room when NPH volunteers, donors and staff work together to continue the legacy Father Wasson founded. In short, it is a culture of love and respect that is given to all.

Father Wasson believed we are all brothers and sisters, and must love each other to accomplish great things. His example of great love is easily applied to all families and how they raise their children. It is the foundation for everyone involved with NPH and how they work together for this common goal. Most importantly, the principle carries forward with the happy children who grow up in an NPH home. They take this love to their communities and countries to make an impact into the future.

In his own words...

So, what is it that makes our children happy? It is, I believe, the balance of four spiritual qualities that have to be applied together. The first of these is love—a specific type of love that the children receive. This is a very important factor in their lives. This kind of love we call security. Our children feel safe because they know that they will not be put up for adoption; that they will never have to leave the home on a certain day or age; that they will never be left to live in the streets; that they belong to and are a part of our family.

They know that their brothers and sisters have a home where they can stay together; that they never again have to witness the death of their mother; that they will never have to withstand neglect and separation or be a burden to their grandparents or aunts and uncles. So, the anguish that children bring with them gradually disappears when they begin to comprehend that they have arrived at their house, that they are safe there and that they will stay there.

There are people who disagree with me on this point. They tell me that it doesn't benefit children to give them too much security, and I agree. But our children have some small insecurities of life in common: Will they have shoes for graduation day? Will they be able to continue with their education in college, university or technical school? And after so many years with us will they find life outside the home to be very difficult?

However, they have basic security. They know that we love them. They know that they can always stay with us. There is no fixed time by which they must leave. They know that the guarantee of their security is love.

In our spiritual formation, we don't put emphasis on ceremonial church. We rather teach the commandments, explain the sacramental system, but above all—above all things—we emphasize the great need to love one another. The word that keeps us together is brotherhood, and every child knows that whatever he does against any person, he does against his brother. We teach, that the worst sin is not being able to live as brothers. Criticizing someone, denigrating someone, denying help to someone, not sharing with those who need you, are all serious sins. I think children recognize this more and more. It is revealed in their confessions, when they feel concerned for hurting or helping someone. Day by day, we talk of brotherhood and try to live it. We remind our children that whatever our race, religion, color, size, intelligence or location in the world, we are all brothers and sisters. Nationality does not create differences—all men are brothers. If we can accept this, then our salvation and our happiness will be assured. This concept is a reality in our family, so much so that it constitutes a criterion for determining what is right and what is wrong.

There are countless stories of how the children who come to NPH overcame unthinkable obstacles, and went on to achieve accomplishments, sharing deep love to change the world. Here is just one . . .

UNCONDITIONAL LOVE
CHANGES
A PEQUEÑO

By: Father Rick Frechette

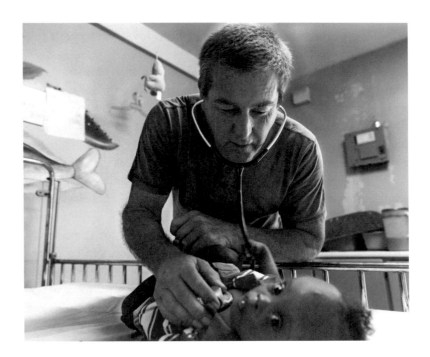

"UNCONDITIONAL LOVE" was not the original phrase used by Father Wasson. He used the Greco-Christian word "agape" as his founding reference, but it would give way to the more familiar expression over time.

Taken from Jesus' teachings on what love is, and elaborated by Saint Paul, "agape" is the highest form of love and means to love freely without expecting anything in return. This means that there is nothing self-serving in your love. But it does not, and cannot, mean that nothing is expected from the person receiving your love.

God's love requires us to be open to love and to be transformed by it.

Dr. Michael Maccoby, who helped Father Wasson articulate the founding values of NPH, draws a parallel between agape, and the definition of friendship offered by the master philosopher-theologian, Saint Thomas Aquinas. "A friend is someone who always wishes you well." This kind of friendship can never do otherwise.

Saint Francis of Assisi captured this virtue in a greeting that was very dear to Father Wasson: Pax et Bonum. This is in fact the motto of NPH (Paz y Bien), meaning "Peace and all good things."

Mature people live with a full awareness of themselves including the parts that are wrong, or in need of ongoing redemption. Similarly, a vibrant place like that of NPH, if mature, also must be able to speak of its failures. These failures, many of which prove temporary, will never be more evident than in the living out of agape.

Neither for Jesus, nor for Father Wasson, could everyone be saved, for the simple reason that agape is not one sided. Agape means, "I offer you, unwaveringly, my love and the love of God, and I am here for you whenever you turn to this love and open your heart." Agape is, often enough, a very tough love.

It can never mean that your love remains silent, and unchallenging, when a person is harming themselves or others. This is in total contrast to wishing someone well. In fact, Father Wasson saw agape as the single value that would define NPH as a family.

I remember the arrival of a family to our NPH home in Haiti in 1988. Four brothers, the oldest of whom would become a phenomenal leader in Haiti, the middle two would also make their positive contributions, and the youngest, whom I will call Marc, would be a terror.

This story does not end poorly. Marc exhibited "agape," finally turning to his love of NPH in the end after much angst.

As a baby, Marc was cared for by Sister Philomena, who would report a strange phenomenon about him as a toddler. If any other toddlers woke up before him, they would not cry or make noise until they saw him awake. It showed, at an early age, his ability to have strong influence over people.

Just like any family can struggle with bad outside influences, NPH has to deal with negative forces such as the Internet, gangs and poverty. Marc became delinquent because of outside influences, and we were frequent targets of his crimes.

Throughout this time, my own love for Marc was very tough. This was necessary, in fact, for both of us. But tough love seemed to do him no good at all. Marc did not alter his language or behavior. I finally refused to speak with him because his conversations were pure bluff to try to get money. Every time I caught him trespassing or stealing, I had him arrested.

In 2013, Marc was about 25 years old and had been involved with criminal gangs in Port-au-Prince. Gang members came to NPH to rob the money that they heard (correctly) was coming with a volunteer from Europe. The robbery took place in our home for the children with disabilities. It became a violent struggle where some of those children were struck, the director of the program was beaten, and the employee who tried to help her was killed. The details are gruesome.

We know firsthand how possible it is to lose influence over young people you have both raised and loved. This is true in any family.

Marc came to see me a day after the crime. His eyes were riveted on the floor as he said to me, "I know I am bad, but I could never be that bad." He wanted to help me catch the culprits, one of whom was his best friend.

Not trusting him, I said, "I saw a movie once where a killer showed up at a police station, offering to help the police find the killer, as a cover-up to his involvement."

Marc stared at the floor. "I had nothing to do with the robbery and killing at the orphanage," he said. "I totally deplore what happened. It was wronger than wrong could ever be."

"I need to ask you two questions. Why would you suddenly show up to offer to help us? How do you expect me to trust you?" I said.

Marc answered, "All these years, I have been knocking at the door the wrong way, and this is the right way."

He explained that since he and his brothers had no other family, NPH is his family, and I was his father. He had no other way to be tied to the home or to my attention except by trouble.

And he wanted and needed to stay tied to us. He desperately wanted to know how he, who had done so much wrong, could return to my favor.

I was astounded, and had to admit to myself that, in fact, it would be difficult for someone who had frazzled me as much as he had, to return to my favor. I felt somewhat ashamed.

"Why are you willing to betray your best friend by helping us arrest him and the others?" I asked. "If you betray your best friend, you can betray me in a minute. You can betray all of us."

He answered, "Betray? I don't understand why you use the word. If your best friend in Connecticut killed someone, would that be fine with you? Would you just leave him in society? He cannot be in society. If you helped to arrest him, for the sake of society, and then helped him to rebuild his life from the inside out, would you consider that betrayal?"

He continued, "If my friend is repentant and open, I will help him. It is not betrayal."

In that moment, I asked Marc to take his eyes off the floor and look at me. For the first time, I told him I was proud of him. We embraced, and from that moment, Marc has been valiant in helping us confront the whole tragic and painful event.

I had never stopped wishing Marc well. I took a strong distance from him in order not to enable or legitimize the harm he was causing himself and others. But when this beautiful day arrived, I was able to forgive. His heart had found the true way to respond to love.

Marc has changed his ways and become an important director in our work with youth. He is focused especially on those who, in his words, are "knocking at our door the wrong way," helping them to find better ways to stay bound to NPH and head toward a brighter future.

FATHER RICHARD FRECHETTE, C.P., D.O.

Born in 1953, Frechette graduated from Assumption College in Massachusetts with degrees in math and philosophy. He attended St. John's University in New York, studied theology as a seminarian, and was ordained a priest in 1979. After a few years as a parish priest in Baltimore, he met Father William Wasson, founder of Nuestros Pequeños Hermanos and worked in Mexico in 1983 at an old hacienda that had been converted to a residential care home for nearly 1,000 vulnerable children. As a priest and administrator, his next calling was to Honduras to help establish a second home for NPH.

Mother Teresa's Sisters of Charity in Haiti directed Father Rick to the next turning point in his life. The sisters were caring for infants born to dying mothers, some sick with AIDS. Many of the babies did not survive, but those who did needed care, love and a place to live. Father Wasson and Father Rick visited Haiti and a children's hospice, and decided to open a new NPH home. Father Rick began servicing at Nos Petits Freres et Soeurs (NPFS, French for "Our Little Brothers and Sisters") and saw the need for medical care. He returned to the U.S. and earned a medical degree in 1998 from the New York College of Osteopathic Medicine and became a general practitioner licensed in New York and Florida.

Today, the doctor-priest leads NPH Haiti's 224-bed, St. Damien Pediatric Hospital, which provides long-term care to critically-ill children, comprehensive maternal care, and outpatient services to over 80,000 children and adults each year. Also, Father Rick advises management and operations of the NPH residential care homes and schools, which serve over 2,000 children. He also founded the St. Luke Foundation for Haiti which creates dignified jobs in social service fields, including over 30 street schools; delivers water to slums, hospitals, and clinics; and buries unclaimed dead from the city morgue.

PRINCIPLE TWO:
SHARING WITH OTHERS

"Truly I tell you, whatever
you did for one of the least of these
brothers and sisters of mine, you did for me."
—Matthew 25:40

IN 2010, an earthquake hit Haiti and in 2015, another hit Mexico. On both occasions, when these tragedies were announced at NPH, the children in the other homes asked to send some of their things to help their NPH brothers and sisters in the country affected by the disaster. They understood their relationship with the children in the nine NPH homes and felt compelled to help.

Sharing is an important part of Father Wasson's philosophy. He knew that people who share are happier and better for it. He wanted his children to grow into generous people who would be compelled to notice others and respond to their needs.

At NPH, the children live a life of sharing. They practice the act every day; they share clothing, they share bathrooms, they share toys, and they share "godparent" sponsors. As their generosity grows, NPH children experience the good feelings created by these actions, and it becomes a deep part of their existence and the culture of the home.

Perhaps a benefit of this sharing philosophy is how it applies to volunteers and donors. As the organization grew, raising funds included the option to sponsor a child as a godparent. This allows sponsors to share in a child's life. Godparents receive letters, grades, photos and information about their godchild. They also have the opportunity to write them, and many even visit their godchild's NPH home. They become part of their godchild's life.

Donors who sponsor programs or support schools also see the direct impact of their generosity. They share in the ongoing success of the program and can visit the NPH home to connect on a deep level to those benefiting from the work.

In his words…
The second principle in the balance of the four
which together constitute our philosophy, another type of
love that children give, is sharing with others.

How do I define the word sharing? How do we practice it in our home? We don't give great importance to memorized and recited prayers because we consider that to be too easy. We believe that a prayer is an action, a good deed done for someone else and to offer this action is an act of kindness to God. This is difficult. It's easier to approach the altar reciting a formula, light a candle and place a flower there and say that that is a prayer.

No. In our family we believe that the only valid prayer is a good deed done for the benefit of another person; that is to see Christ in our brother and serve Him through our neighbor.

Our older boys formed a musical group and this group goes to the penitentiary of the State of Morelos (Mexico) to play and sing for the prisoners. After the concert, these young men meet with the inmates, chatting with them and listening to their problems. A similar thing is done in the home for the elderly in Cuernavaca and in the hospital for those with incurable illnesses, in Texcoco.

Another group of our boys accompany our volunteer nurse to visit a school/home in a very rural area, where they tend to the children of poor subsistence farmers. There, our children share their food, medicine; they give classes in hygiene to the children, they help them with the cleaning and encourage them to study.

Not a day goes by without the poor coming to our door: hungry children; a sick grandmother; an alcoholic; a young mother abandoned with a hungry baby in her arms and another two or three little ones pulling at her skirt. Whichever one of our young men answers the door, attends to the needs of these people as best he can. He simply goes to the kitchen to get some food and gives it to the hungry; gives used clothing to those who are half-naked, gets vitamins for the sick or helps the old grandmother return to her hut.

This manner of sharing helps our children avoid seeing themselves as the center of the universe or as believing that the whole world revolves around them. It's better to see that the world revolves around others. That is the reason why sharing is such an important part in our balance of four principles. With the guarantee of security and without sharing anything, the children could become vain, spoiled and selfish. But when we are insisting that you share what you have with others, a balance is achieved.

The child who feels insecure and full of anguish feels a tremendous need to be compensated by the possession of material things. He finds it very difficult to share these things or do away with them. But once the children are with us, even though they bring memories of devastating experiences (some of our children have seen their parents murdered, have lived in the street for many years, have been victims of inhuman cruelties and severe neglect) they gradually realize that they are safe at NPH. Once you feel safe, you are ready to share.

I've never met a happy person who does not share. I have met many different people who have amassed huge fortunes and are willing to share because they give money, but they just do it and avoid paying taxes. Certainly, this is better than doing nothing. Others spend their lives accumulating things and money, and when they die, they inherit it all to their relatives or to persons designated by the state, and never know the joy of sharing what they had with the poor.

What is sharing? I think it's giving something that one has, quietly and humbly to someone who needs it. It may not be money. Maybe it's time. Time is something that not *many people want to share. They may say—time is money and it's easier to share a little bit of money instead of time. However, I believe that sharing includes giving our time, our advice, our knowledge, our clothes, our food, our money to those who really need it.*

I have found that people who share are the most responsible people. And I don't mean responsible only for themselves. What I mean is that they have a sense of responsibility towards humanity. Responsible people, for example, don't give donations to an unknown cause. They investigate carefully what percentage of the collected funds are allocated to managers and what percentage is used for the poor, whose cause is being used for promotion. After researching dozens of charities, they will find one or two that according to their research, are doing a good job and optimally using the donations they receive. Then, these responsible donors generously share their money with them.

Some believe that rich people must learn to share, but this action has nothing to do with social status or wealth. It's about each of us. Everyone has to learn to share and the more you can share, the happier you will be.

Father Wasson's sharing principle changes not only the children in the homes but sponsors, donors and all those connected to NPH. When donors visit a home, they share in the happiness of the NPH children, see the impact of the programs reaching out to those in desperate need and then carry that experience back. Donors, godparents and staff alike have a much greater sense of sharing by being part of the NPH family. They come to understand the great impact Father Wasson's principle of sharing has on changing the lives of families—both the NPH family and their own.

SHARING STORIES
Sonia, Merlin and the
Pequeños and Pequeñas

By: Reinhart Koehler

I DO NOT KNOW of any family, small or large, where sharing is so ingrained in the family members' behavior. Take Sonia, a 13-year-old girl from the NPH home in Honduras. At a special dinner night, the dessert was a very delicious, albeit small cookie. Our table had a cookie left over, and I gave it to Sonia who sat at a table next to ours. I thought she would just pop the morsel into her mouth. But as she turned towards her table, without thinking she split the cookie into four equal parts, sharing it with the other pequeñas.

Sharing gestures like these are common occurrences in the daily life of the children. Every month, the children who are celebrating their birthday go into town where they can purchase a small gift and afterwards are treated to a special meal. Almost everyone will wrap some of his/her food into a napkin and bring it home to share with a friend.

Last Christmas, I participated in the pre-Christmas celebration of the "Hogar" San Francisco, which is much like our "secret Santa." A group of 12 young boys had drawn names written on small pieces of paper and were opening their presents. When I saw what kind of gifts the boys gave to the one they had drawn, my jaw dropped. Each one had taken his most prized possession and wrapped it to give to the other boy. I was immediately reminded of the Bible story of the widow's mite (Mark 17:7-16), who gave away her last two pennies. The sharing among the children also illustrates the meaning of the gospel story where Jesus feeds 5,000 with two fish and five loaves of bread (John 6:1-14). The children have few possessions yet through sharing, everything they have seems to be enough for everyone, even in the toughest times.

Of course, sharing is not only giving of material things. Sharing can be act of kindness because we acknowledge the other person and express that we care about them. We share when we give of ourselves through service, when we assume responsibility for someone, when we sit down and listen to their joys and sorrows. Through sharing, the pequeños and pequeñas bond and ultimately create and cement strong caring relationships among each other. Together, they form an extended family in which they grow into service-oriented adults, always ready to give a helping hand to those in need.

Dr. Merlin Antúnez was a seven-year-old boy when he arrived with the first four children at the home in Honduras. He is a good example of what Father Wasson considered success of our work. Today, Merlin is an orthopedic surgeon. However, what really makes him a success is the way he cares about his patients, how he will go out of his way to find a solution for everyone. No matter how big the challenge, he is kind to them and helps them not only through his outstanding medical skills but by making sure they can come to the surgery center and have adequate care afterwards. If they need to stay for aftercare and there is no place for them to stay, he will find a place for them and pay for it. He puts his caring attitude into action through sharing.

In my 38 years with NPH, I continue to be amazed by both the readiness with which the pequeños and pequeñas share, and the joy they find in sharing. Of course, the children also know that the NPH family can only exist because of the generosity of others, the desire of so many to share with them even though most do not even know them personally. In the end, everybody learns that when sharing is carried out with joy and love, the reward is happiness.

REINHART KOEHLER

Reinhart joined NPH Mexico as a volunteer in August 1982. At the time, Mexico was the only NPH home. Though he had signed up for only a year, his involvement with NPH turned out to be a lifetime commitment. He has a master's degree in education from the University of South Carolina and studied Educational Leadership at the University of San Diego. He has served the NPH family in multiple roles over the years. He spent extensive time with Father Wasson, helping him and Frank Krafft of Our Little Brothers and Sisters with their initial fundraising efforts in the German speaking countries of Switzerland, Austria and Germany. Reinhart also worked closely with Father Wasson when he and Father Rick Frechette helped found NPH Honduras in 1985. He also assisted in establishing NPH homes in other Central American countries.

Reinhart serves on various boards guiding the NPH family locally and internationally. He enjoys being with both his small family (wife Nohemí and two adult children, Camila and Jan) and his big NPH family; watching and supporting the children grow into the wonderful adults God intended them to be.

PRINCIPLE THREE: WORK

"Among the purposes of a society,
must be that of foreseeing
a continuous source of work
at all times and all ages."
—Leo XIII Rerum Novarum

FATHER WASSON'S BELIEF in work was key to how his children would make an impact in the world. The concept of work is a basic fundamental to the kids of NPH. They are expected to contribute no matter their strengths, weaknesses, or capabilities. They are not afraid of hard work and understand the importance of their contributions to the success of the NPH family. This principle prepares them to enter the world as adults and become productive members of society.

In his words...

The children hate to be called "supported" by other people. They prefer to stand on their own and be a valuable element for the family. Once our children understand that we are a family and not an institution, they want to participate in the effort to make it progress. Therefore, work is a vital factor of our philosophy.

NPH musical groups travel to the United States each year to perform and raise money for the organization. In each city they visit, families host pairs of children during their stay. The children have a wonderful opportunity to see how these families live. But as with so many things about NPH, the impact is almost always more profound for the members of the host families.

NPH staff always hear comments from families about how they loved having the kids in their homes. How helpful they were. The families talk about how the visit had a tremendous impact on their own children. The experience creates an understanding of NPH, influences their children's actions to help, and showcases the incredible change NPH has made on the lives of these once disadvantaged children.

Families notice the strong work ethic of NPH children. The dishes don't stay on their table, but rather are carried and rinsed in the kitchen. The kids make their own beds, and you won't see clothes on the floors or furniture because they are always folded and put away.

In his words...

The third principle in the balance of four is an old deed that we call work. We don't hire other people to do our work. We do it ourselves. We do the cleaning of the house; we prepare our meals; we wash, iron and mend our clothes; and we do our own construction and maintenance. Our young men dig the foundations, cut the wood, mix the cement and do everything except the technical aspects of new construction. Also, they tend to the livestock, milk the cows, clean the stables and pig-pens, cultivate the fields of our farms, and supervise their little brothers. Our young ladies tend to the babies and the kindergartners.

We are often asked how we develop the habit of work in our children. First, we let them know that the work is often unpleasant.

Every one of the children at NPH has to dedicate at least one hour a day to work. This is above and beyond the time they spend in school, the time for homework, the time dedicated to other activities like music, theater or sports, as well as the time it takes to make their beds and wash and iron their clothes. The older children have to dedicate two hours a day for work and the young adults assigned to our offices dedicate 3–4 hours a day for work. Even our little ones have tasks. Give them an old rag and teach them to clean something. Then when they grow, their chores grow with them. They learn to clean windows, sweep floors, clean bathrooms. Whatever task is assigned, they know they have to do it and to do a good job.

It's not necessary that the adults do the house work for the children. That's absurd. The children have to do their appropriate chores. There is no reason for voluntary workers to make them food, sew, wash or iron their clothes or serve them in any way. Teach them, yes. Supervise them, yes. Listen to them, advise them and love each and every one of them, yes. But to do their chores? No! An important aspect of sharing, work and responsibility for our kids is made as the older ones care for the younger ones.

Children who do these chores (all chores are assigned on a rotating basis) learn to use the bathroom more carefully and advise their brothers to do the same. All of our children have to do chores that they don't want or like, however, we insist that they have to, and so from an early age they learn the habit of work.

At NPH, children give back service years prior to high school and college. They assist in caring for their family members and are role models, guiding their brothers and sisters and serving as examples of future possibilities.

Once again, this simple principle can be integrated in the lives of all families. NPH donors and sponsors who know the organization will tell you that Father Wasson's principles changed the way they raise their children for the better. For all of us, contributing to something bigger than ourselves makes us happier.

THE HARD WORK OF LETICIA

By: Father Phil Cleary
Past International Director, NPH &
Current Chaplain NPH Mexico

IN MEXICO, poverty has ravaged families for generations. In 1999, completely by accident, a team from NPH stumbled upon a group of people in a "shack village" living at a dump. We realized all these families were surviving on trash, and raising children in abject poverty. None of the children were ever able to attend school.

Their "homes" were made of metal and materials from things thrown away. The families spent their time picking through garbage, surviving off what they found and recycling junk. One such family was Leticia's. She grew up living in a shack with her mother and siblings. Her father was long gone and her mother had never learned to read or write. The only way she could care for her children was to scavenge for whatever she could find in the wretched mountain of trash.

Leticia (Lety) and her sisters supplemented the family income by picking through the garbage as well.

The NPH leaders knew we had to create a program for the children and families living in the dump. We decided to have a meeting with the whole community. After we had presented our ideas, Lety gave us a hard time…apparently lots of do-gooders had come through promising the world and never delivered. Lety and a friend of hers grilled us and wrote us off saying that we would be the same.

But it wasn't only Lety and her friends NPH would have to convince. It was a sacrifice for the families to let their children come to school because that meant fewer hands working the garbage.

Lety was on one of the first busses that arrived at NPH. They would start a program to provide education and reach out to the community from our home in Mexico. We bussed Lety, and over one hundred like her, back and forth from the garbage dump every day. The program would give these children an education, treatment for lice, medical and dental care, and two decent meals each day. The new students were provided two uniforms—one which they wore home each day and one they would leave behind. The children living at NPH in their year of service washed the other one so it would be clean to put on when they arrived again the next day. On arriving, the children took a shower (most had no running water), put on their clean uniform and headed to school.

When Lety first arrived, she had dark blotches all over her skin and orange hair. These are classic signs of malnutrition. But as time passed, her nutrition improved and a beautiful young woman emerged. Soon, her strong personality drove her to study and work hard at school.

Lety was the first person from that horrid place to ever finish high school. I remember the look of pride on her face as she walked to get her diploma in her cap and gown.

But Lety would not stop there. Because of her work ethic and study habits, NPH put Leticia through the university, where she received a degree in psychology. After graduation, she went to work as a school psychologist.

Lety had two dreams in her life—one of serving other needy children, and another of saving enough money to move her mother and sisters off of the garbage dump. She was able to achieve both. Today, her mother and family have moved into a real home and Lety continues to work with children, giving back to help others strive for greatness in their lives.

Father Wasson's philosophy of work allows each child to contribute to their home and empowers them to reach for their dreams. At NPH we teach our children, both those living in our homes and those in our schools, that working hard is the cornerstone to success...just like Lety.

FATHER PHIL CLEARY

Father Cleary was born on September 5, 1953, the second of seven children to Virginia and Francis Cleary. He was raised in a middle-class Irish neighborhood on the north side of Chicago, attended Catholic schools and Chicago seminaries, and graduated with degrees in psychology and theology. During his time in the seminary, he worked as a counselor for five years at a Chicago orphanage, as a dorm director at a home for delinquent and troubled youth, and spent three years as the youth minister at a city parish.

Father Phil was ordained a priest of the Archdiocese of Chicago on May 9, 1979, and assigned to a poor inner-city parish in a Mexican-Puerto Rican neighborhood on the city's west side. Three years into his assignment at that parish, Father Phil was elected to the board, and later appointed chairman, of the Association of Chicago Priests. Shortly after that, he was elected to the Board of Directors of the National Federation of Priests' Councils, representing all of the priests of the state of Illinois.

Quite by accident, Father Phil learned of Nuestros Pequeños Hermanos from a fellow priest who had visited the orphanage in Mexico. In 1983, Father Phil volunteered to work at the orphanage for a summer. Soon he received permission from his bishop in Chicago to serve at NPH and in 1984, that three-month term of volunteer work became a life-time commitment to the poor, orphaned and abandoned children of NPH.

Father Phil began his service to NPH as Chaplain to the children and as Father Wasson's adviser. His presence in Mexico gave Father Wasson the freedom to extend his vision of service to children in other countries. Father Phil later served for 10 years as National Director for NPH Mexico and then for 10 years as President of NPH International. He has now gone back to his roots and spends his time as chaplain, priest and father to the children in Mexico, living in the main home of NPH Mexico.

PRINCIPLE FOUR: RESPONSIBILITY

*"Human life is the answer to reality.
Being responsible is when we want to
respond to another human being."*
—William McNamara, OCD

MOST CHILDREN WHO enter NPH have tragic life stories. From a tender age, they have witnessed terrible events, experienced suffering and lacked the basic necessities most people take for granted. The concept of responsibility, and acceptance of this fourth principle, can blossom only after a solid foundation of love and security has been built.

Those who spend time with the NPH children watch the transformation of new pequeños from their first day to becoming part of the family. It takes time for them to understand their new life at NPH, accept love and begin to share. The concept of assuming the responsibility is an important part of becoming a productive member of the family.

Children soon become proud of their home, their brothers and sisters, and their belonging to the NPH community. As children graduate and move out in the world, they continue to proudly refer to themselves as "pequeños" and part of the "NPH family." Donors and sponsors refer to themselves in a similar manner.

The concept of being responsible—for your actions, your family, how you represent NPH in the world—is vitally important in the future success and accomplishments of NPH children. It's this acceptance of responsibility that allows them to hold their heads high and reach for opportunities that seemed unimaginable without a secure foundation.

In his words...

The fourth principle in the balance of four is that which we call responsibility and co-responsibility. We have never had written laws or rules at NPH. Yes, we have verbal agreements and the understanding of these agreements is that every one of our children will be responsible at all times for their own actions and words. We call attention from time to time about conduct.

If I, for example, encounter garbage thrown on the ground and I see one of our kids stepping on it, or around it, I call his attention to it and let him know that even though it is not his task, he has to either pick it up or find out who is responsible for it and get them to pick it up.

Our experience has been, with some of our children, that they really like responsibility and can't wait to exercise it. Perhaps to them it implies a certain power or prestige. Others evade responsibility and they don't want to be involved. Therefore, on the one hand we need to channel those who seek responsibility and, on the other hand, strengthen that capacity for those who evade it.

When we see a child so terribly hurt by tragedy, who cannot speak or communicate with anyone and arrives here and begins to understand that he is surrounded by security and love, and then he relates to his brothers and sisters, shares his life with them and takes his studies seriously because he can see a future, we feel extremely happy.

I think through the understanding we have with our children, they know that we want them to be responsible at all times. They try to be, and if they are not, I ask them why.

And once more, just as between security and sharing there has to be some balance, there also has to be a balance between work and responsibility. A child that is taught to work, to keep their mouth shut and just keep on working, that child simply becomes automated like a robot. He never asks questions, never challenges anything, never does anything except what he is commanded to do—and that is not good. We have discovered that it is better that the child can speak without fear of repercussions. If he has a logical motive to protest, he should be allowed to do so. They will learn the reasons behind everything.

All children in Nuestros Pequeños Hermanos know that they are loved, and that everyone here gives their time, their energy and their life to try solving their problems and assure they have a better future.

At NPH, responsibility is shared among all the children. Not only are they given assignments but they understand the collective work is shared amongst many. By becoming role models, the children express themselves and share their talents within the NPH family. They give back service years, becoming role models to their younger siblings. These qualities provide the foundation for a responsible life for our children as they go into the world as adults.

In his words...

Lead by example, that's important, more important than anything you can say about sharing. In Nuestros Pequeños Hermanos, we talk about sharing, because we constantly mention and promote it. I cannot force one of our boys to lend his best shirt to a brother, or to help another with his homework, and yet this way of sharing occurs constantly in our home. Those who don't share or don't want to, see the example and are impacted favorably. Moreover, we go outside the home to share: our children visit prisons, hospitals, nursing homes and orphanages. They bring their guitars and the folk ballet group performs. While some play and dance, others spend time with the patients, the elderly, and children. People come every day and knock on our doors, poor people with hunger, and our kids share their food with them.

This is not going to solve the world's hunger, not even in our neighborhood, but our children learn compassion and responsibility.

MY STORY OF RESPONSIBILITY

By: Miguel Venegas
Executive Director, NPH

I AM MIGUEL VENEGAS. Today, I am the Executive Director of NPH but the story of my life would not be the same without Father William Wasson and his vision for creating a family to raise children in need. I am a product of the NPH philosophy developed by our beloved Father Wasson.

In many ways, my story is a typical NPH kid's story. I arrived at the NPH home in Mexico in 1984 at the age of 15 with my two siblings, Luis and Laura. My life, up to that point, was sad but common. My mother died when I was just eight years old and as you can imagine, my four siblings and I were devastated. So was my father. He was not able to cope with the pain and took refuge in alcohol. It left my oldest sister, who was 15 years old at that time, in charge. She took on the role of mother in almost unbearable circumstances. After three years, I don't know what evils got into my sister's head, but she committed suicide. I wish we could have done something to avoid this tragedy, but I have come to understand the difficulty of managing depression.

Once again, we suffered devastation as my father became an alcoholic and was not able to take care of any of us. Luis, Laura and I suffered hunger, poverty, and many times had no place to stay. Seeing us on the streets, neighbors called the authorities to help us and the social workers sent us to an orphanage. My other sisters, Olga and Maria, didn't join NPH because they were 17 and 18 at the time and decided to stay with my father to care for him. The first place wasn't helpful and we were mistreated, so we were sent to another orphanage where mistreatment happened again. Throughout this time, my grandmother, who was unable to take us in, was looking for solutions. She found NPH.

NPH was more than home, it was a family. Not only were we given the basic needs of food and shelter but, as a part of a bigger family, we came to understand that our contributions mattered. I was provided a safe environment, an education and unconditional love. I was also given responsibility for the first time. We were required to have chores, wash our own clothes and keep the house clean even when no one asked us to do so. Having these responsibilities helped me and the other children build self-esteem. This affected my educational and work trajectory. I began to understand that I was responsible in my own actions and choices in life. I remember Father Wasson was always thinking of ways to develop our skills for the future.

Over time, I learned to care for others. I learned to be accountable for chores or duties assigned, and how those responsibilities affected those around me.

NPH is the best thing that ever happened to me. This sense of responsibility had a profound impact on my life and ultimately, led me back to my NPH family.

Father Wasson was a visionary leader. He saw the potential of pequeños and gave them positions of responsibility. And these pequeños responded well to this sense of contributing to something bigger. Father Wasson was preparing us to live in our communities, take care of our basic needs and to be leaders in our society. We were able to accomplish that through the value of responsibility.

I took advantage of all the opportunities NPH offered. I was able to go to the U.S. to study English and then continue to study at the University of Texas. After I graduated with a degree in computer science and a minor in mathematics, I came back to Mexico to complete my third year of service. It is an important responsibility for me (and all pequeños) to give back to the home that had provided me with so much.

Once I finished my year of service, I started my independent life. I got a job at a prestigious company, and started a business executive career and a new life.

When I was offered an opportunity to go back to NPH to help, it was a difficult decision for me. I wanted to break the cycle of poverty and ignorance. And I was doing that exactly.

After much discernment, I decided to give up my career in business because I am eternally grateful for the opportunity I was given during my upbringing at NPH. I realized the values of Father Wasson were deeply rooted in me and my decision making. I wanted to respond to the need, to contribute to this great NPH family that supported me when I was desperate.

I went back to NPH to help Father Wasson open a home in Guatemala. After I helped establish that home, I moved back to Mexico to help the management team. I believe the sense of responsibility and how I responded to the needs of the family contributed to my promotions from one job to another until I was appointed Executive Director.

I'm very proud of the work we do and the thousands of children that we help.

When I became Executive Director, I promised that I would continue to make a difference and protect the rights of the children in our care. I have also had to respond to the worldwide movement of deinstitutionalization and creating opportunities to reach children beyond our NPH homes. We have partnered with United Nations task forces locally and embraced a number of sustainable development goals. Our NPH One Family program is an example of how we are transforming the way we care for children. The foundational support we offer is no longer limited to kids who live inside an NPH home. Whether a child lives with NPH or lives in a nearby community with parents and relatives, we help them.

In 65 years, a lot has changed. We have changed the physical structure of the typical NPH home. Today, kids live and play in small, family-style groups. They have stronger bonds with caregivers trained in positive discipline and social-emotional learning concepts. But our fundamental values remain the same as we create a sense of family, of belonging and of permanence for each child.

The next 65 years will see us continue to bring Father Wasson's philosophy forward to meet new challenges. Our focus will still be the children. Taking the best care of them possible and meeting their needs. We will always look for new and better ways to support kids. Kids with big dreams—just like me.

MIGUEL VENEGAS, NPH EXECUTIVE DIRECTOR
Miguel graduated from secondary school and then completed his year of service to the NPH family at the home in Miacatlán. Miguel then was given the opportunity to attend the unique English program in Yarnell, Arizona. He earned his bachelor's degree in Computer Science with a minor in Mathematics from the University of Texas at Tyler.

After college, Miguel worked at American Express until Father Wasson asked him to return to NPH and run the newly opened NPH home in Guatemala as the administrator and accountant. After two years in Guatemala, Miguel returned to Mexico to develop the Finance Department of NPH International, where he served as Director of Finance for six years. In 2009, Miguel became Executive Director of NPH International.

Miguel earned his MBA from the world's leading international business school, Thunderbird University School of Global Management in 2014.

Miguel is based out of NPH International in Cuernavaca, Mexico. He is a member of the NPHI International Board, NPHI Finance Committee and NPH USA Board. He and his wife, Maria, have three children—Alain, Andrea and Miguel.

AN EXTRA PRINCIPLE: ACHIEVING AN EDUCATION

"Prove me, O God, and know my heart:
examine me, and know my paths.
And see if there be in me the way of iniquity:
and lead me in the eternal way."

—Psalms 138:23-24

ALTHOUGH LIFE IN Father Wasson's family was built on the four principles described, he also believed that education was the only way to overcome poverty and change the future for his children. Once a child's basic needs such as food, clothing and shelter are met, and they feel secure, they can begin to dream and see their potential. That potential will only be reached with the opportunity of an education.

In his words…

Education will take my children out of the poverty into which they were born.

The masses will be exploited until the educational level increases. Illiterates—people who cannot read or write—have little hope of reaching a standard level of living in a world that becomes more complex every day.

Each of the NPH homes is dedicated to providing a quality education. Beyond the importance of educating the NPH children, the NPH schools reach out to children in the surrounding communities. Transportation and enrollment allow these children to gain an education and work toward a better future. All of the homes offer the opportunity to attend high school. If the home is not able to have the high school on campus, the children stay in an NPH house near the local high school so they can attend.

As the children age, they are offered opportunities for training, vocational school and university. In fact, in most countries, the rate of NPH students who graduate high school and the rate of attending college is higher than the national average.

In his words...

Since the beginning we have made every effort to have a good academic program. Initially, we had all the children in one room where a volunteer teacher taught the classes from first to fourth grade, but we have grown and our educational program has improved.

When a child is receiving a good education, he or she feels confident, not only in the present but even with respect to the future, knowing that he is ready to face it.

In addition to complying with all regulations, we try to add cultural courses that are not mandatory but very enriching experiences, such as music, folkloric dance and theater.

With very few exceptions and some of these for special reasons, our young men and young women usually study to become teachers. Why? Because the biggest need in Latin America is good teachers; teachers who not only know but feel, that can see the problems and human needs.

But even if our children receive the best academic education, their professional career has to start from the bottom and they will need to climb up only by their own efforts. Our pequeños have to make their way in life for themselves, obtaining and maintaining a job based solely on their own merits.

When our children leave the home, they are prepared, they have received a good education and a positive family environment thanks to the time they have been with us. Still, adjusting to the outside world is not easy. Because of the education they have had, they manage to adapt and realize that the habit of sharing is a virtue that must be retained in their lives and in the life of their family.

Perhaps the greatest evidence of NPH's success through education are the stories from former pequeños. Many have achieved success; some with careers in the community and others returning to NPH to make an impact back in the homes as directors, managers and teachers. These role models empower the children; providing a roadmap to success.

THE STORY OF EDUCATING JULIO

By: Bishop Ronald Hicks
Auxiliary Bishop of Chicago

FATHER WASSON BELIEVED that education provides the key ingredient to break the chain of poverty. Our children at NPH have the opportunity to study not only until high school graduation, but also to continue through vocational school or the university, if they can persevere and make the grade. Depending on their abilities and determination, our children have gone on to become teachers, doctors, accountants, chefs, welders, bakers, nannies, lawyers and even logistical engineers. This story is about Julio Arevalos who graduated as a logistical engineer.

In 2001, after his biological family was no longer able to care for him, Julio arrived at NPH El Salvador. He was 11 years old. Julio's personality reflects a soul which is gentle, humble and kind. However, scratch the surface and his intellectual curiosity and determination shines.

At age 16, Julio asked me, "Padre Ron, what did you have to do to earn a master's degree and a doctorate?"

"Julio, I was just in the right place at the right time. I got lucky."

He was having none of it. Julio looked at me unconvincingly and responded with a slight grin, "Oh, I think there was a little more than luck involved."

Our children at NPH are the lucky ones. They are blessed with access to an academic system to which many in their countries could never have. However, they need to make the most of this educational gift. Julio did just that.

He graduated with honors from NPH's elementary and junior high school and then was lauded as a top academic student in high school. Julio earned a scholarship to study engineering at the Central American Institute of Technology (ITCA).

While studying at ITCA in La Union, El Salvador, he embraced the NPH values and ordered his life daily to not only study, but also to pray, ride his bike, play soccer, cook meals and keep his small room neat and tidy. The habits and rules from his NPH family carried through to everything in his life including his studies.

Once I visited him in the summertime and was overwhelmed by the tropical temperature and humidity. I remember asking him, "How are you surviving this oppressive heat?"

"I sleep on a hammock so that my sweat drips onto the floor instead of into a mattress," he answered pragmatically. "Don't worry about me, Padre, I am fine."

This was Julio's trademark. No matter the adversity or obstacle he encountered, he not only survived, but found ways to thrive.

Growing up at NPH, Julio was surrounded by volunteers, donors and visitors who spoke English. Like so many of our children, he made the most of every encounter by asking questions. "How do you say, THIS or THAT in English" or "What does that mean?" Julio not only studied English, but he immersed himself to become fluent in both the written and spoken language.

Beyond English, his leadership skills were also honed during his one-year term as a member of the fifth cohort of NPH's Leadership Institute in Seattle, Washington. Julio utilized all he had learned at NPH through his education and all the values of NPH to obtain a job and begin a successful career. Julio and his family now live in San Salvador, where he works in the technical support department for AT&T.

In 2016, I was honored to baptize Julio and Carolina's baby. After the ceremony, he reminded me that during my time at NPH El Salvador, I was not only a friend and spiritual father to the pequeños, but also a mentor, teaching by example. I am so proud of Julio and what he represents for future pequeños and everyone in the NPH family.

Father Wasson made education one of his core values because he knew it was the way to truly empower the children to be agents of change in their own countries. Through access to good education, NPH has changed—and continues to change—the lives of countless children for the better. Like Julio, it gives NPH children options in their lives. In other words, by investing in the pequeños' education, we contribute not only to their happiness and well-being, but also to making their country and our world a better place.

RONALD HICKS
Auxiliary Bishop of Chicago

Bishop Ron Hicks was born on August 4, 1967 and raised in South Holland, a suburb of Chicago. After graduating from college in 1989 with a B.A. in Philosophy, he left for Mexico and volunteered at NPH for one year. Upon his return he entered the major seminary and was ordained a priest on May 21, 1994 for the Archdiocese of Chicago. He ministered in a variety of parishes and then served as the Dean of Formation at St. Joseph College Seminary and also at Mundelein Seminary. In 2003, he earned the Doctor of Ministry Degree from The University of Saint Mary of the Lake.

In July 2005, with permission from Francis Cardinal George, he moved to El Salvador to begin his five-year term as Regional Director of NPH in Central America where he was affectionately called, "Padre Ron."

On September 17, 2018, he was ordained a Bishop by Blase Cardinal Cupich at Holy Name Cathedral, Chicago.

NUESTROS PEQUEÑOS HERMANOS

*"For I was hungry and you gave me food,
I was thirsty and you gave me drink,
a stranger and you welcomed me."*
—Matthew 25:35

AT ITS CORE, NPH is an organization that supports orphaned, abandoned and disadvantaged children in Bolivia, the Dominican Republic, El Salvador, Guatemala, Haiti, Honduras, Mexico, Nicaragua and Peru by raising them in a permanent environment to help break the cycle of poverty. NPH has raised over 20,000 children since the mid-1950s, changing their lives and helping them become leaders in their own countries.

In a changing world, countries have looked to NPH to increase services and reach out to communities with programs for those in need. Just as Father Wasson did, NPH has answered the call. The organization has expanded educational opportunities for non-resident children, provided healthcare resources and delivered countless other services, reaching over 170,000 children and families living in poverty.

The needs are much greater than they were in 1954. Issues of poverty, natural disasters, government unrest, homelessness, HIV/AIDS, and overall dangerous conditions in Latin American countries make the work of NPH more important and more challenging than ever. Over 13 million children have been orphaned by HIV/AIDS. About one million children are exploited annually in the multibillion-dollar sex industry. Approximately 246 million children are engaged in exploitative child labor; 75% of them in hazardous environments. In Latin America alone, over 40 million children live in extreme poverty.

Thanks to the financial support of donors, NPH continues to reach the underprivileged in Latin America and the Caribbean. Driven by the core principles of Father Wasson, NPH has established a reputation for quality care and created a culture of family both inside and outside the homes.

Father Wasson passed away on August 16, 2006. He was not only revered by his NPH family but recognized worldwide as the recipient of many awards including:

- Luis Elizondo Humanitarian Award—1977
- Good Samaritan Award from the National Catholic Development Conference—1979
- Franciscan International Award—1981
- Order of the Aztec Eagle—1990
- National Caring Award by the Caring Institute of Washington, D.C.—1997
- KFC's Colonel's Way Award—1998
- El Sol de Nuestra Communidad Award—1998
- Kellogg's Hannah Neil World of Children Award—2000
- Jefferson Award for Public Service—2003
- Ivy Humanitarian Award by the Ivy Inter-American Foundation—2005
- Opus Prize Finalist—2005

Through all his accolades and achievements, Father Wasson remained humble. Perhaps his legacy is best summed up by a simple and beautiful quote he spoke often...

> *"You may only be one person in the world, but you may be all the world to one child."*

In his words...

I've always believed that we have a destiny in this life and perhaps our greatest prayer is the one that accepts that fate. The words, "Thy will be done" in the Lord's Prayer mean that we must accept what comes to us as an important thing in God's plan, even though at that time we may not be able to understand, appreciate and evaluate it. For me this is the biggest problem, I am always trying to anticipate what God wants, because I know that true collaboration with God's will is to use our intelligence and ability to do what we believe we must do. If what we are trying to do is not possible, or we are not able to accomplish this, we must also accept it with confidence and not with frustration or rebellion. In other words, I think we do the best we can and accept the outcome as God wanted it to happen.

I think all good deeds are prayers because they are acts of love and any act of love is a communion with God.

I want NPH to grow and withstand. I am making all possible arrangements for that. But I believe in God and if in His power and wisdom He wants it, then He will find people capable to continue this work.

Father William Wasson

BE PART OF THE NPH FAMILY

Anyone involved with NPH will tell you they receive more than they give. NPH offers donors an extraordinary opportunity to affect change by connecting with the homes, the children, the programs and the community at large.

Support for NPH means an opportunity to break the cycle of poverty. It means raising leaders in their own countries. It means NPH can offer community services to reach those in desperate need.

- **Choose a country**—Provide support for a home or community
- **Choose education**—Sponsor a technical school or university scholarship or support an NPH primary school
- **Choose a program**—Community programs serve thousands of people each year

Your contribution will empower children with life-changing opportunities. In return, you will see the impact of your support. We invite you to join the NPH family. To love, to share, and to work with us toward a better future for those in need.

How to Donate:
NPH USA
134 North La Salle Street, Suite 500
Chicago, IL 60602-1036
1-888-201-8880

www.nphusa.org

THE HOMES OF
NUESTROS PEQUEÑOS
HERMANOS

NPH MEXICO

Opened: August 2, 1954

The first home, NPH Mexico is housed in a converted sugar plantation which serves as the main facility for the large family of children. Always bustling with activity, the home's facilities are quite extensive and offer a small-town feel with cobblestone streets.

Services include:
- Casa San Salvador, Miacatlán: NPH Mexico's main facility since 1970
- Casa Buen Señor, Cuernavaca: NPH's Bachillerato Tecnológico—technical high school
- Monterrey and Mexico City: Youths attending universities
- Ciudad de los Niños ("City of the Children") in Matamoros, founded by John Shinsky

NPH BOLIVIA

Opened: April 16, 2005

Casa Padre William B. Wasson is the newest NPH home. Located in the lowlands near Santa Cruz de la Sierra, it features family-style homes, a primary school, dining hall, garden and clinic. The weather in Bolivia is hot, humid and rainy so the housing was renovated with durable roofs, windows and walls to be more secure.

The NPH Bolivia home includes a primary school, clinic, farm, and fully independent water system. Food sustainability is important to the home and production here includes:
• Yucca and rice
• Milk
• Fish
• Meat from cows and goats

NPH DOMINICAN REPUBLIC

Opened: January 6, 2003

Our family in the Dominican Republic began with seven children in a rented home in the town of San Pedro de Macoris and quickly expanded to six houses. The Bishop of San Pedro de Macoris, Francisco Ozoria Acosta, donated land to NPH on behalf of his diocese. Two adjacent parcels were then purchased and in September 2005, the family moved into its new home, naming it Casa Santa Ana. The home has a Montessori program, a special education program and a vocational school offering technical careers in:

• Cabinetmaking
• Handicrafts
• Shoemaking
• Sewing
• Clay
• Music

NPH EL SALVADOR

Opened: June 29, 1999

Father Wasson founded the sixth NPH home in Santa Ana, El Salvador. As with the other NPH homes, his decision was based on the needs of the many neglected and abandoned children. In December 2004, the last of the buildings in Texistepeque were completed and the family moved into its new home, Casa Sagrada Familia ("Holy Family").

The home has a primary school for kindergarten through grade nine and a residential house in Santa Ana for pequeños to live while in high school. Students can attend vocational studies including carpentry, tailoring, welding, and baking. There is also a scholarship to allow children from the local community to attend school. A daycare center, opened in 2017, serving children from the local community.

NPH GUATEMALA

Opened: November 11, 1996

NPH's fifth home for orphaned, abandoned and at-risk children was established in rented facilities in 1996. The family moved to its new home, named Casa San Andres, in August 2003, situated 4,900 feet above sea level in Guatemala's highlands near Antigua.

Along with a school and vocational program, NPH Guatemala has two special projects, a family bakery and The Smile Shop. The bakery offers fresh pastries made on site and coffee to help with fundraising. It is staffed by students who gain professional experience and business management skills. The Smile Shop is an integrated learning store for those with physical and cognitive disabilities.

NPH HAITI

Opened: October 14, 1987

The NPH Haiti home is also known as Nos Petits Frères et Soeurs (French for "Our Little Brothers and Sisters"). Two years after the home opened, Father Wasson and Father Rick Frechette established a medical program which would become St. Damien Pediatric Hospital. (See next page)

Programs:
- St. Hélène Foyer, the main children's home
- Kay St. Germaine, Kay Gabriel and Kay Elaine are rehabilitation outpatient centers
- Father Wasson Angels of Light home and school for vulnerable and displaced children
- Don Bosco higher education program

NPH ST. DAMIEN PEDIATRIC HOSPITAL, HAITI

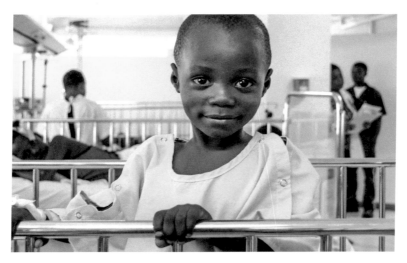

Opened: 1989

St. Damien Hospital is the premier pediatric hospital in Haiti and provides high-quality medical treatment for disadvantaged and sick children. More than half of all patients are admitted for an infectious disease such as tuberculosis, malaria, and HIV while 25 percent are admitted for non-infectious diseases such as cancer, cardiovascular disease, and kidney infection. Most patients admitted are also malnourished. The outpatient clinic treats 100 children daily. St. Damien Pediatric Hospital and associated public health and community programs provide over 80,000 services to children and adults annually.

NPH HONDURAS

Opened: May 24, 1986

A thriving, bustling community, Rancho Santa Fe is the second oldest of the NPH homes. The boys and girls make their home in this vast wooded oasis in the hills—a metropolis in comparison to the surrounding quiet pueblos—while older children study and live in Tegucigalpa. A new home in Catacamas serves children transitioning into stable, long-term living environments.

NPH Honduras has a program called Chicas Poderosas focused on girls' empowerment. The program supports over 100 young women at the main home and in the nearby community, engaging them in diverse activities meant to build self-confidence and leadership skills.

NPH NICARAGUA

Opened: May 10, 1994

Casa Padre Wasson has been the main home near Jinotepe since 2011. Prior to that time, the main home was on Ometepe Island in Lake Nicaragua. Seismic and volcanic activity on the island in 2005 led to the acquisition of new property on the mainland where Casa Padre Wasson was built. High school and university students live and study in Managua, the capital city.

NPH Nicaragua includes vocational workshops and a farm where the children help raise fruits and vegetables as well as chickens, pigs, cows and fish. There is a wastewater system that works without electricity or chemicals, with the treated water used for irrigation. Approximately 500 solar panels were placed on building rooftops to achieve greater self-sufficiency in energy costs. The Samaritan Project provides occupational and physical therapy, psychological care, and medical exams for children in the local communities of Jinotepe and Ometepe Island.

NPH PERU

Opened: October 6, 2004

Casa Santa Rosa is the NPH home in San Vicente de Cañete. The home was originally located in Cajamarca in the northern Andes Mountains, about 13 hours by car from Lima, the capital. In 2007, it was moved to Lunahuaná, approximately 115 miles (185 km) from the capital. The home occupied rented facilities until property in San Vicente de Cañete was acquired and Casa Santa Rosa was completed in 2011.

NPH Peru operates a bakery as a vocational workshop to teach a valuable trade as well as provide bread for the home. Agriculture is another vocational training program for the children. Corn is harvested as feed for livestock and to generate income for the home.

ABOUT THE AUTHORS

BISHOP RONALD HICKS & MARLENE BYRNE

BISHOP RONALD HICKS is the Vicar General of the Archdiocese of Chicago. He became involved with NPH following his college graduation when he volunteered at NPH Mexico for one year. After being ordained a priest, he served in the Archdiocese of Chicago. In 2005, he began serving as Regional Director of NPH in Central America. He was consecrated a Bishop in 2018.

MARLENE BYRNE has worked her entire career in advertising and has authored six books. She became involved with NPH at her parish and met Bishop Ron during the fiesta tour with the music group from El Salvador. Her family hosted two of the dancers and she fell in love with the mission of NPH. She served on the Midwest Board of Directors for NPH USA and was asked to host a pequeño from El Salvador while he received a series of treatments at Shriners Hospital of Chicago to repair a severe cleft palate. Over the years, the two became friends and their love of NPH inspired them to publish Father Wasson's writings in this book.

ALL of the proceeds of this book are being given directly to NPH USA for future children.

Contributors: Thank you to Father Phil Cleary, Father Rick Frechette, Miguel Venegas and Reinhart Koehler who provided stories of children who grew up at NPH, lived by Father Wasson's philosophy, and went on to achieve success.

"The most important thing for me is that my children practice charity, because if they love they will be loved too. This will make their work efficient and effective. They will have a great influence on their own children, in society and they will reach their own salvation."

"Lo más importante para mi es que mis niños practiquen la caridad, porque si aman serán amados también. Esto hará que su trabajo sea eficiente y efectivo. Tendrán una gran influencia en sus propios hijos, en la sociedad y alcanzarán la salvación."

Father William Wasson